ZRJC
4 / 12

W9-BIK-684

Backyard Animals
Prairie Dogs

Megan Kopp

www.av2books.com

Go to **www.av2books.com**, and enter this book's unique code.

BOOK CODE

P 6 2 4 4 5 6

AV² by Weigl brings you media enhanced books that support active learning.

AV² provides enriched content that supplements and complements this book. Weigl's AV² books strive to create inspired learning and engage young minds in a total learning experience.

Your AV² Media Enhanced books come alive with...

Audio
Listen to sections of the book read aloud.

Key Words
Study vocabulary, and complete a matching word activity.

Video
Watch informative video clips.

Quizzes
Test your knowledge.

Embedded Weblinks
Gain additional information for research.

Slide Show
View images and captions, and prepare a presentation.

Try This!
Complete activities and hands-on experiments.

... and much, much more!

Published by AV² by Weigl
350 5th Avenue, 59th Floor
New York, NY 10118
Website: www.av2books.com   www.weigl.com

Library of Congress Cataloging-in-Publication Data

Kopp, Megan.
 Prairie dogs / Megan Kopp.
   p. cm. -- (Backyard animals)
 Includes index.
 ISBN 978-1-61690-624-5 (hardcover : alk. paper) -- ISBN 978-1-61690-630-6 (softcover : alk. paper)
 1. Prairie dogs--Juvenile literature. I. Title.

 QL737.R68K67 2011
 599.36'7--dc22

                    2010045180

Printed in the United States of America in North Mankato, Minnesota
1 2 3 4 5 6 7 8 9 0   15 14 13 12 11

052011
WEP37500

Editor Heather Kissock   **Design** Terry Paulhus

Contents

Meet the Prairie Dog

Prairie dogs are **mammals** that belong to the **rodent** family. They can be found living on the grasslands of western North America.

A prairie dog is about the size of a rabbit. Prairie dogs have long sleek bodies, light-brown fur, and short tails. Like all rodents, prairie dogs have strong front teeth that are growing all the time.

Prairie dogs are social animals. They live in family groups called coteries. Their homes are underground and are made up of rooms and tunnels.

Several coteries can live in one area. Together, they form a prairie dog town. A town can have more than one hundred prairie dogs in it.

Prairie dogs were named by French explorers. They called them *petit chiens*, or "little dogs."

Prairie dogs often greet each other with a kiss or nuzzle.

All about Prairie Dogs

There are only five **species** of prairie dogs in the world. All species look alike, but each species has slightly different features. The two most common prairie dogs are the black-tailed and the white-tailed.

Adult prairie dogs can weigh up to 3.7 pounds (1.7 kilograms). Most range from 11 to 13 inches (28 to 33 centimeters) in length. Their tails can be 1.2 to 4.7 inches (3 to 12 cm) long.

Prairie dogs bark at each other when danger is near.

Where Prairie Dogs Live

Black-tailed Prairie Dog

Found in the central part of the United States and Canada

Mexican Prairie Dog

Found in northeastern Mexico

White-tailed Prairie Dog

Lives in the western United States

Gunnison's Prairie Dog

Lives in the southwestern United States

Utah Prairie Dog

Found in south-central Utah, in the western United States

Prairie Dog History

Rodents can be grouped into more than 30 different families. Prairie dogs belong to the squirrel family.

Prairie dogs have been on Earth for a long time. **Fossils** of prairie dogs have been found that are about 2.6 million years old.

The prairie dog is known as a keystone species. This is a species that other animals depend on for their survival. At least nine species of animals, including the swift fox and the golden eagle, depend on prairie dogs for their survival.

Prairie dog fossils have only been found in North America.

In the 1800s, explorers Lewis and Clark wrote about prairie dogs in their journals.

Prairie Dog Shelter

Prairie dogs dig long **burrows**. Up to 500 pounds (227.3 kg) of dirt is moved for each burrow they dig. Prairie dogs spend much of their time building their burrows and keeping them tidy.

A burrow can have several entrances. The prairie dogs use their sharp claws to move dirt out of the holes into tall piles near an entrance. The piles give the prairie dogs a high spot to watch for **predators**. They also protect the burrows from flooding after a heavy rain.

Inside the burrow, there are separate bedrooms, nurseries, and bathrooms. Burrows average 16 to 33 feet (5 to 10 meters) long. They can extend 6.5 to 10 feet (2 to 3 m) into the ground.

Each entrance has a special room near it. Prairie dogs use these rooms to listen for danger.

A burrow is home to only one prairie dog family. A family is made up of a male, two to four females, and their young.

Prairie Dog Features

All prairie dogs share the same basic features. Their bodies are specially **adapted** to living in open grassland areas. Their strong back legs allow them to stand upright. They can then watch for predators using their excellent eyesight.

CLAWS AND PAWS

A prairie dog's paws are small. They are used to pull plants from the ground and hold food. The paws have long claws at the end. These claws are sharp and curved for digging.

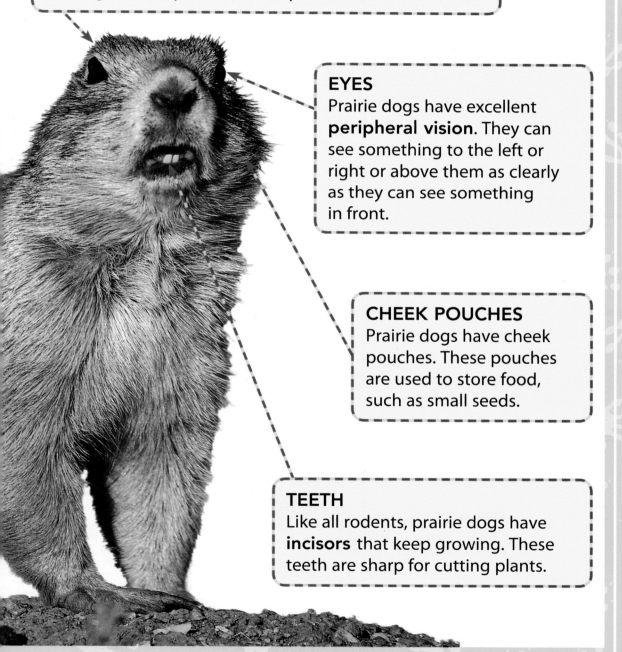

EARS
A prairie dog's ears are small and rounded. They sit back on the head and fold over the ear opening. This keeps dust and dirt from entering. Prairie dogs have excellent hearing. This helps them avoid predators.

EYES
Prairie dogs have excellent **peripheral vision**. They can see something to the left or right or above them as clearly as they can see something in front.

CHEEK POUCHES
Prairie dogs have cheek pouches. These pouches are used to store food, such as small seeds.

TEETH
Like all rodents, prairie dogs have **incisors** that keep growing. These teeth are sharp for cutting plants.

What Do Prairie Dogs Eat?

Prairie dogs are mainly **herbivores**. They eat grasses and the leaves, stems, flowers, and seeds of small plants. Prairie dogs sometimes eat grasshoppers, beetles, and other insects.

Prairie dogs will chew down all the tall plants around their burrow. This gives them a clear view of possible predators.

Dried food is often stored in the prairie dog's burrow.

Prairie dogs do not need to drink water. They get enough water from the leafy foods they eat.

Prairie Dog Life Cycle

Prairie dogs mate in early spring. After one month, the female gives birth to an average of three to four pups. Prairie dogs grow fast. In one year, they become adults.

Birth

Prairie dog young are called pups. At birth, pups are blind and hairless. They stay in the burrow under their mother's care for the first six weeks of their lives. They are then **weaned**, but remain close to their mother for at least two more weeks.

Six Weeks to One Year

At about six weeks of age, prairie dogs begin leaving the burrow for short periods. Over time, they spend more time outside the burrow. By six months, prairie dogs are considered full grown. However, they will remain with their family until the females give birth the next spring.

Prairie dogs have a short lifespan. Black-footed ferrets, hawks, eagles, and snakes all hunt prairie dogs. Most adults live only three to four years.

One to Two Years

At one year of age, young prairie dogs begin leaving the family burrow to find their own territory. By two years of age, they have families of their own.

Encountering Prairie Dogs

Prairie dogs live in areas that are known to be good farmland. This can create problems for farmers. If the farmer is raising cattle, the prairie dogs compete with the cattle for grass to eat. If the farmer is growing crops, the prairie dogs will sometimes eat the plants that are being grown. Some farmers take extreme steps to rid prairie dogs from the land. This affects prairie dog populations and the animals that rely on prairie dogs.

Two species of prairie dog are currently **endangered**. These are the Mexican prairie dog and the Utah prairie dog. Being put on the endangered list saved the Utah prairie dog from **extinction**. People cannot hunt animals that are endangered.

Some prairie dogs carry diseases that can be passed along to humans.

In the 1970s, there were fewer than 4,000 Utah prairie dogs in the world. Today, there are more than 50,000.

Myths and Legends

American Indians have many myths and legends that involve prairie dogs. The Navajo believe that, at one time, prairie dogs were people who lived in caves. They would invite people into their homes and then steal from them. One of the Navajo gods became angry. He entered their caves and turned them into the small rodents they are today.

In other American Indian stories, the prairie dog is portrayed as being easily fooled. The Apache, however, have several myths in which prairie dogs have special powers.

The Apache's traditional lands are located in the southeastern United States.

A Prairie Dog Legend

This Apache legend is about a woman saved by prairie dogs.

A woman was traveling back to her people. It was the middle of winter. She was cold, hungry, and far from home. She came to a prairie dog town. The prairie dog people took pity on her and invited her in. A prairie dog woman rubbed her hand on the burrow's wall, and a small bit of food appeared. The visitor ate and ate, but the food remained the same size. She took a small cup of water and drank. The cup remained full. The prairie dog man gave the visitor crushed grass to keep her warm for the rest of her journey home, but he refused to give her any of the prairie dog power. He said that she had given her children bows and arrows to hunt prairie dogs. He did not like that, so he would not share the power.

The woman returned home, but she did not tell anyone of her encounter with the prairie dogs. She hoped that she might still get some of their powers. She never did.

Frequently Asked Questions

Are prairie dogs and gophers the same animal?

Answer: No. Prairie dogs belong to a different family than gophers. Prairie dogs are ground squirrels. They are more closely related to chipmunks than gophers.

When are prairie dogs most active?

Answer: Prairie dogs are diurnal. This means they are most active during the day. Prairie dogs spend most of their day looking for food. At night, they rest in their burrows.

How many entrances does a burrow have?

Answer: A prairie dog burrow will have at least one entrance. Most burrows have five or six entrances. One researcher discovered several Utah prairie dog burrows with 29 entrances.

Words to Know

adapted: adjusted to the natural environment

burrows: holes or tunnels dug in the ground

endangered: in danger of no longer living on Earth

extinction: no longer living any place on Earth

fossils: traces of an animal that are left in a rock

herbivores: animals that eat mainly plants

incisors: long, sharp teeth at the front of a prairie dog's mouth

mammals: warm-blooded animals that have a spine, fur or hair, and drink milk from their mother

peripheral vision: outside the direct line of sight

predators: animals that hunt other animals for food

rodent: a group of mammals that includes rats, mice, beavers, and rabbits; known for growing sharp front teeth for gnawing

species: animals that share certain features and can breed together

weaned: stopped from drinking a mother's milk

Index

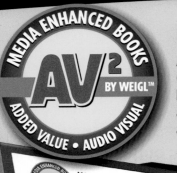

Log on to www.av2books.com

AV² by Weigl brings you media enhanced books that support active learning. Go to www.av2books.com, and enter the special code found on page 2 of this book. You will gain access to enriched and enhanced content that supplements and complements this book. Content includes video, audio, web links, quizzes, a slide show, and activities.

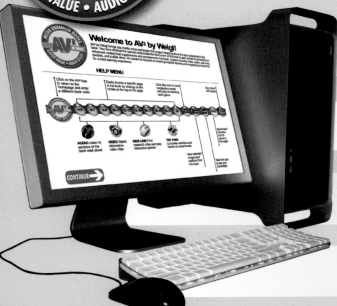

Audio
Listen to sections of the book read aloud.

Video
Watch informative video clips.

Embedded Weblinks
Gain additional information for research.

Try This!
Complete activities and hands-on experiments.

WHAT'S ONLINE?

Try This!	Embedded Weblinks	Video	EXTRA FEATURES
Identify different types of prairie dogs.	More information on identification.	Watch a video about prairie dog behavior.	**Audio** Listen to sections of the book read aloud.
List important features of prairie dogs.	More information on the history of prairie dogs.	See a prairie dog in its natural environment.	**Key Words** Study vocabulary, and complete a matching word activity.
Compare the similarities and differences between young and adult prairie dogs.	Complete an interactive activity.		**Slide Show** View images and captions and prepare a presentation.
Test your knowledge of prairie dogs.	More information on encountering prairie dogs.		**Quizzes** Test your knowledge.
	More stories and legends.		

AV² was built to bridge the gap between print and digital. We encourage you to tell us what you like and what you want to see in the future.
Sign up to be an AV² Ambassador at www.av2books.com/ambassador.